## HAL•LEONARD

### Jazz Play-Along

Book and CD for B♭, E♭, C and Bass Clef Instruments

Volume **90**

**Produced by Don Sickler**

T0042551

10 TIME-HONORED TUNES

Cover photo © William Gottlieb / Retna Ltd.

ISBN 978-0-7935-8760-5

## HAL•LEONARD®
### CORPORATION

7777 W. BLUEMOUND RD. P.O. BOX 13819 MILWAUKEE, WI 53213

Visit Hal Leonard Online at
**www.halleonard.com**

# THELONIOUS MONK CLASSICS

## Volume 90

## Produced by
## Don Sickler

### Featured Players:

**Don Sickler–Trumpet**
**Ronnie Mathews–Piano**
**Kiyoshi Kitagawa–Bass**
**Ben Riley–Drums**

## Recorded, mixed, and mastered by Rudy Van Gelder, Van Gelder Recording Studio, Inc.

### HOW TO USE THE CD:

Each song has <u>two</u> tracks:

#### 1) Split Track/Melody

**Woodwind, Brass, Keyboard,** and **Mallet Players** can use this track as a learning tool for melody style and inflection.

**Bass Players** can learn and perform with this track – remove the recorded bass track by turning down the volume on the LEFT channel.

**Keyboard** and **Guitar Players** can learn and perform with this track – remove the recorded piano part by turning down the volume on the RIGHT channel.

#### 2) Full Stereo Track

**Soloists** or **Groups** can learn and perform with this accompaniment track with the RHYTHM SECTION only.

# MONK'S DREAM

BY THELONIOUS MONK

CD
1: SPLIT TRACK/MELODY
2: FULL STEREO TRACK

C VERSION

# ASK ME NOW

SOLO
Ⓓ Gm7  C7  F#m7  B7  Fm7  Bb7  Em7  A7  Ebm7  Ab7

B7b5  Bb7  Eb7  D7  DbMAJ7  Eb7(#11)

Ebm7  Ab7(b9)  |1. B7b5  Bb7b5  A7b5  Ab7b5  |2. B9  C7(b9)  Db  Ⓓ

Ⓔ Ebm7  Ab7  DbMAJ7  Ebm7  D9(13)  DbMAJ7

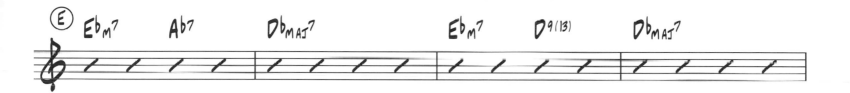

Eb7  Ebm7/Ab  Ab7  Gb7

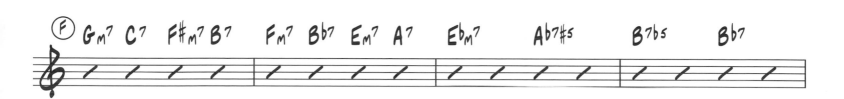

Ⓕ Gm7  C7  F#m7  B7  Fm7  Bb7  Em7  A7  Ebm7  Ab7#5  B7b5  Bb7

D.S. AL FINE

Eb7  D7  DbMAJ7  Eb7(#11)  Ebm7  Ab7(b9)  B9  C7(b9) Db  Ⓓ

# EVIDENCE

BY THELONIOUS MONK

**5** : SPLIT TRACK/MELODY
**6** : FULL STEREO TRACK

C VERSION

SOLO (3 CHORUSES)

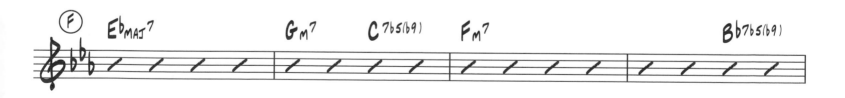

D.S. AL FINE
(AFTER 3RD CHORUS)

# THINK OF ONE

BY THELONIOUS MONK

C VERSION

MEDIUM SWING
INTRO (SOLO BASS)

\* THE 4-NOTE PATTERNS (8TH NOTES) HAVE A MORE EVEN 8TH NOTE FEELING.

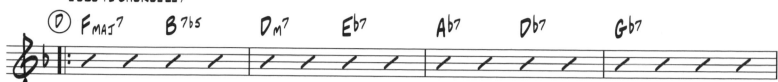

SOLO (2 CHORUSES)

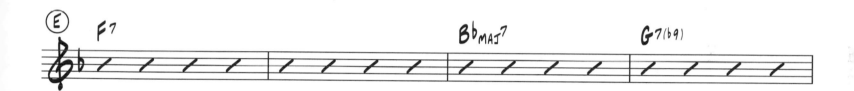

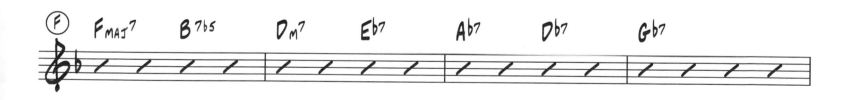

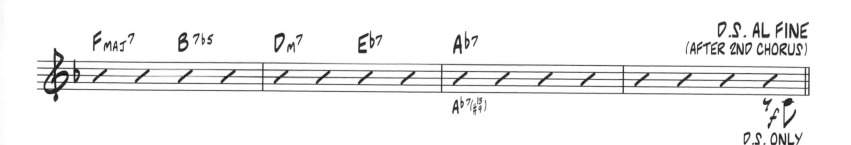

# REFLECTIONS

BY THELONIOUS MONK

C VERSION

* MONK'S "BENT" NOTE

# STRAIGHT NO CHASER

CD
11 : SPLIT TRACK/MELODY
12 : FULL STEREO TRACK

BY THELONIOUS MONK

C VERSION

# COMING ON THE HUDSON

CD
13 : SPLIT TRACK/MELODY
14 : FULL STEREO TRACK

BY THELONIOUS MONK

C VERSION

# BRAKE'S SAKE

BY THELONIOUS MONK

CD
⟨15⟩ : SPLIT TRACK/MELODY
⟨16⟩ : FULL STEREO TRACK

C VERSION

# BA-LUE BOLIVAR BA-LUES-ARE
## (BOLIVAR BLUES)

BY THELONIOUS MONK

CD
17 : SPLIT TRACK/MELODY
18 : FULL STEREO TRACK

C VERSION

# GREEN CHIMNEYS

BY THELONIOUS MONK

C VERSION

MEDIUM UP SWING
INTRO (SOLO PIANO)

PIANO PLAYS 1ST 8 MEASURES OF Ⓐ FOR THE INTRO

Ⓐ PLAY
Ab m

Ⓑ Gb7    Cb7    Gb7    Cb7

Gb7    Cb7    Gb7    Cb7

Ⓒ Ab m

1. TO SOLO        2. LAST TIME    Db7(#11)

SOLO (3 CHORUSES)
Ⓓ Ab m

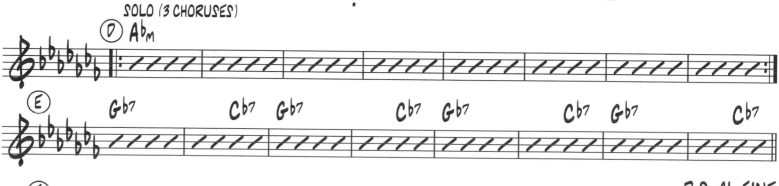

Ⓔ Gb7    Cb7  Gb7    Cb7  Gb7    Cb7  Gb7    Cb7

Ⓕ Ab m                                  D.S. AL FINE
                                        (AFTER 3RD CHORUS)

# MONK'S DREAM

BY THELONIOUS MONK

Bb VERSION

**CD**

◆❸ : SPLIT TRACK/MELODY
◆❹ : FULL STEREO TRACK

# ASK ME NOW

BY THELONIOUS MONK

Bb VERSION

**CD**

5 : SPLIT TRACK/MELODY
6 : FULL STEREO TRACK

# EVIDENCE

BY THELONIOUS MONK

**Bb VERSION**

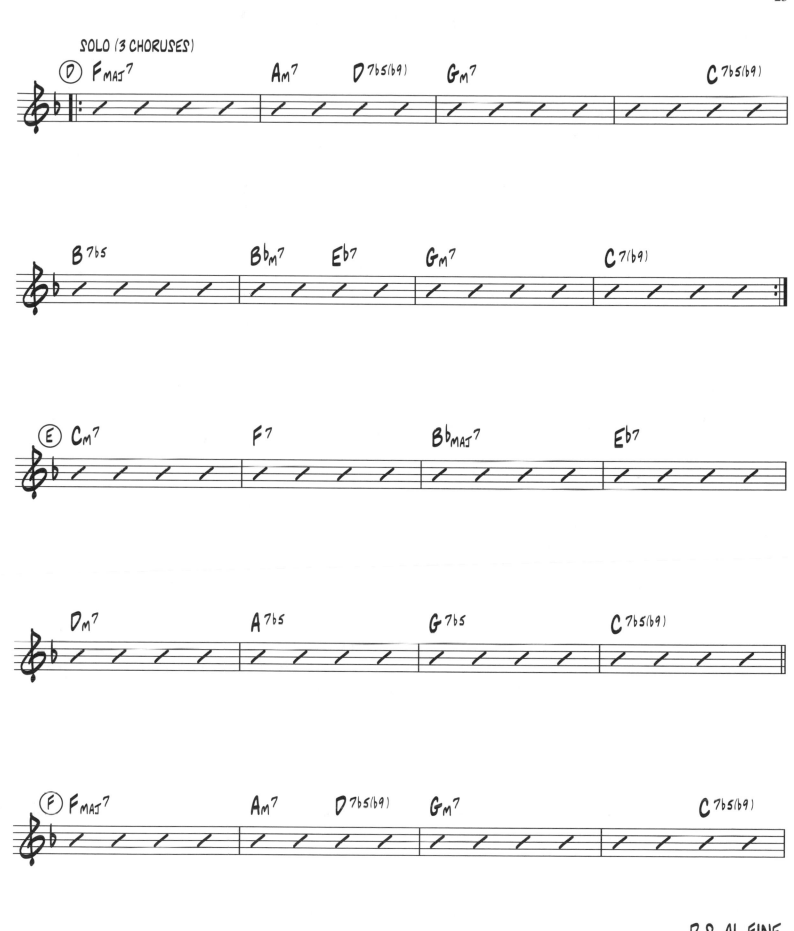

# THINK OF ONE

BY THELONIOUS MONK

CD

■ **7** : SPLIT TRACK/MELODY
◆ **8** : FULL STEREO TRACK

**Bb VERSION**

\* THE 4-NOTE PATTERNS (8TH NOTES) HAVE A MORE EVEN 8TH NOTE FEELING.

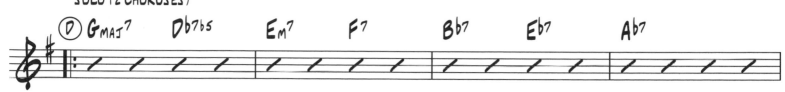

SOLO (2 CHORUSES)

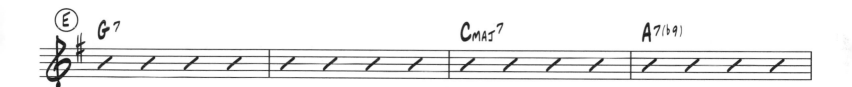

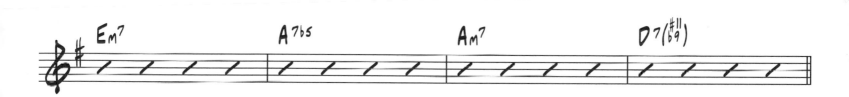

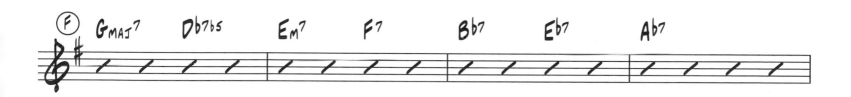

# REFLECTIONS

BY THELONIOUS MONK

**CD**
**9** : SPLIT TRACK/MELODY
**10** : FULL STEREO TRACK

**Bb VERSION**

\* MONK'S "BENT" NOTE

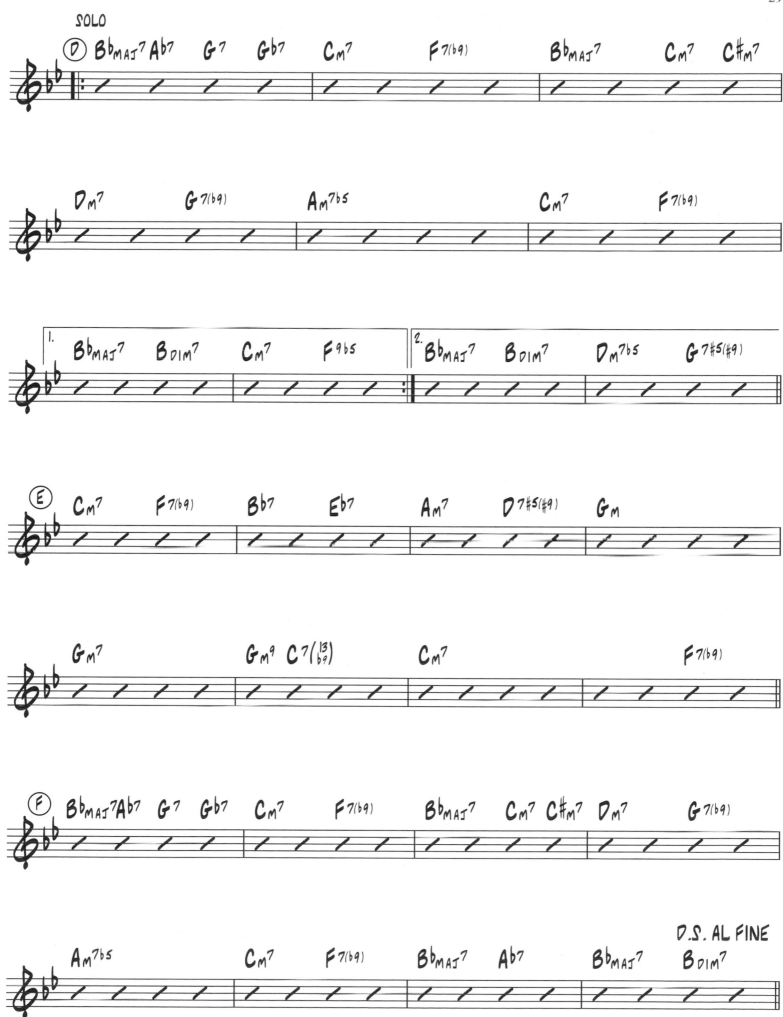

# STRAIGHT NO CHASER

CD
◆11: SPLIT TRACK/MELODY
◆12: FULL STEREO TRACK

BY THELONIOUS MONK

**Bb VERSION**

MEDIUM BLUES

SOLO (8 CHORUSES)

D.S. AL FINE
(AFTER 8TH CHORUS)

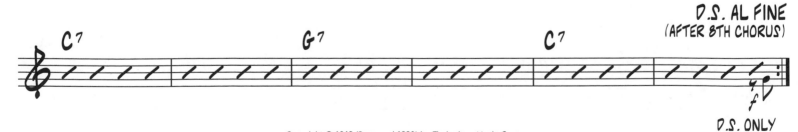

D.S. ONLY

# COMING ON THE HUDSON

BY THELONIOUS MONK

Bb VERSION

**CD**

: SPLIT TRACK/MELODY
: FULL STEREO TRACK

# BRAKE'S SAKE

BY THELONIOUS MONK

**Bb VERSION**

MEDIUM SWING
INTRO (RHYTHM SECTION)

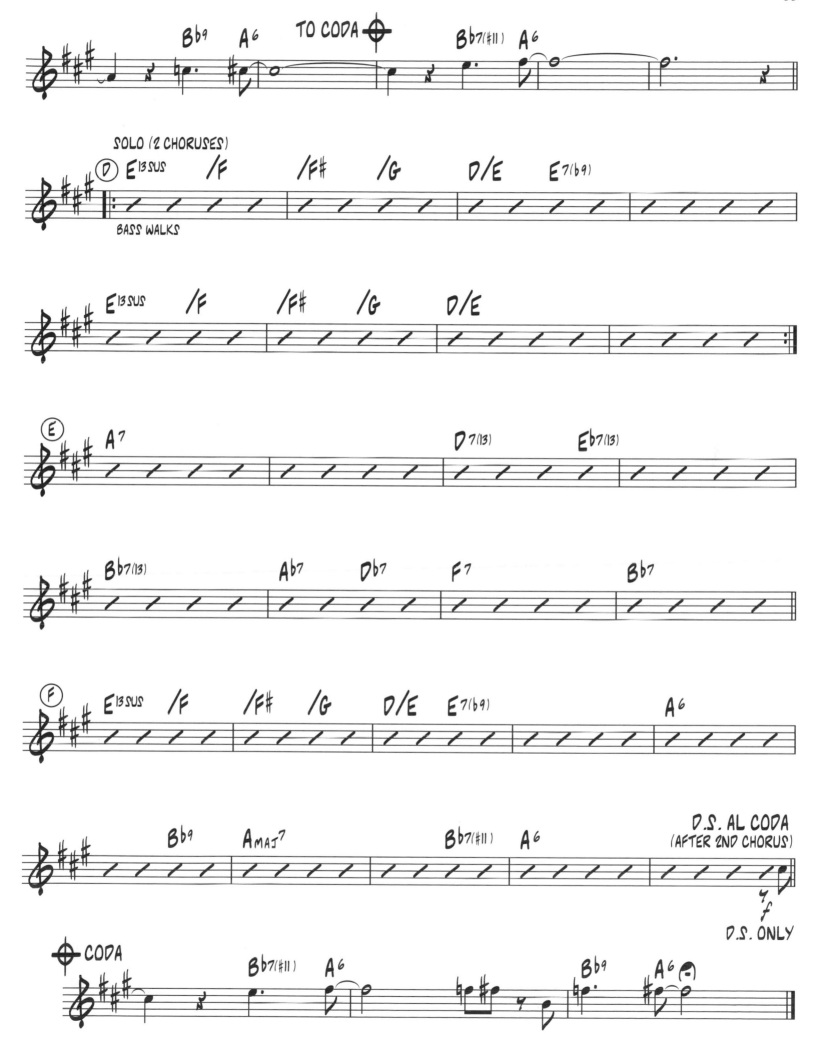

# BA-LUE BOLIVAR BA-LUES-ARE
## (BOLIVAR BLUES)

**Bb VERSION**

BY THELONIOUS MONK

# GREEN CHIMNEYS

BY THELONIOUS MONK

Bb VERSION

# MONK'S DREAM

CD
1: SPLIT TRACK/MELODY
2: FULL STEREO TRACK

BY THELONIOUS MONK

Eb VERSION

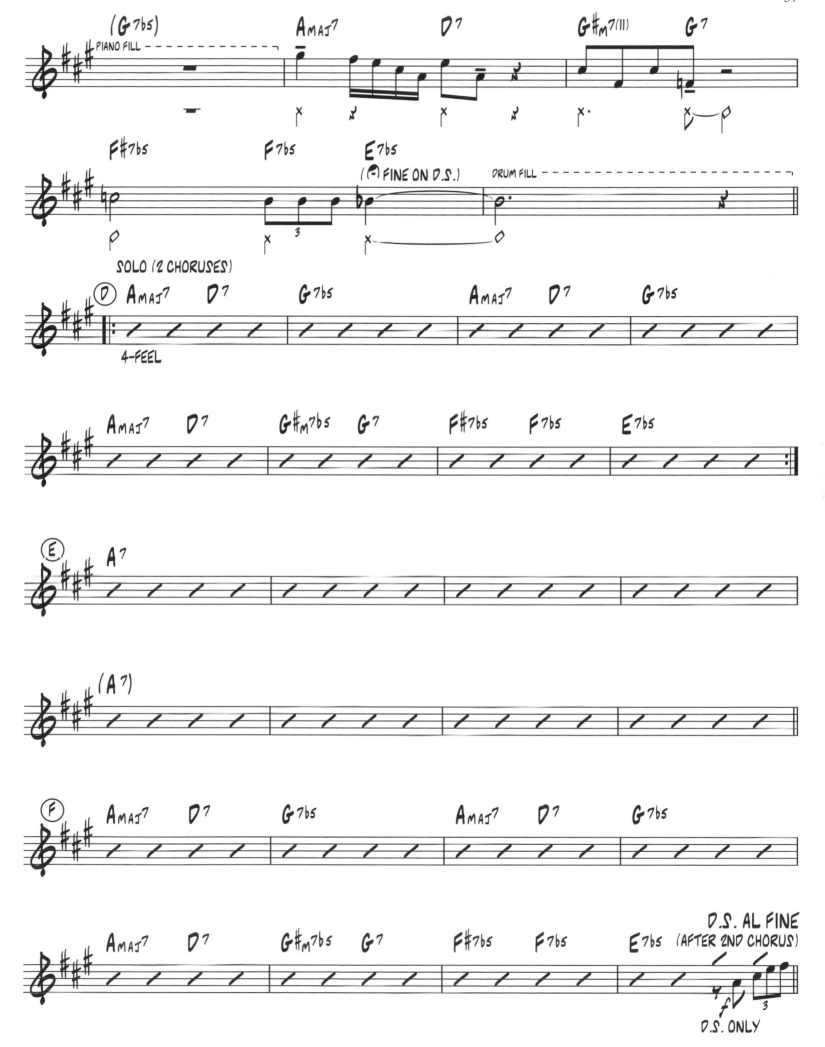

**CD**

◆ 3 : SPLIT TRACK/MELODY
◆ 4 : FULL STEREO TRACK

# ASK ME NOW

BY THELONIOUS MONK

Eb VERSION

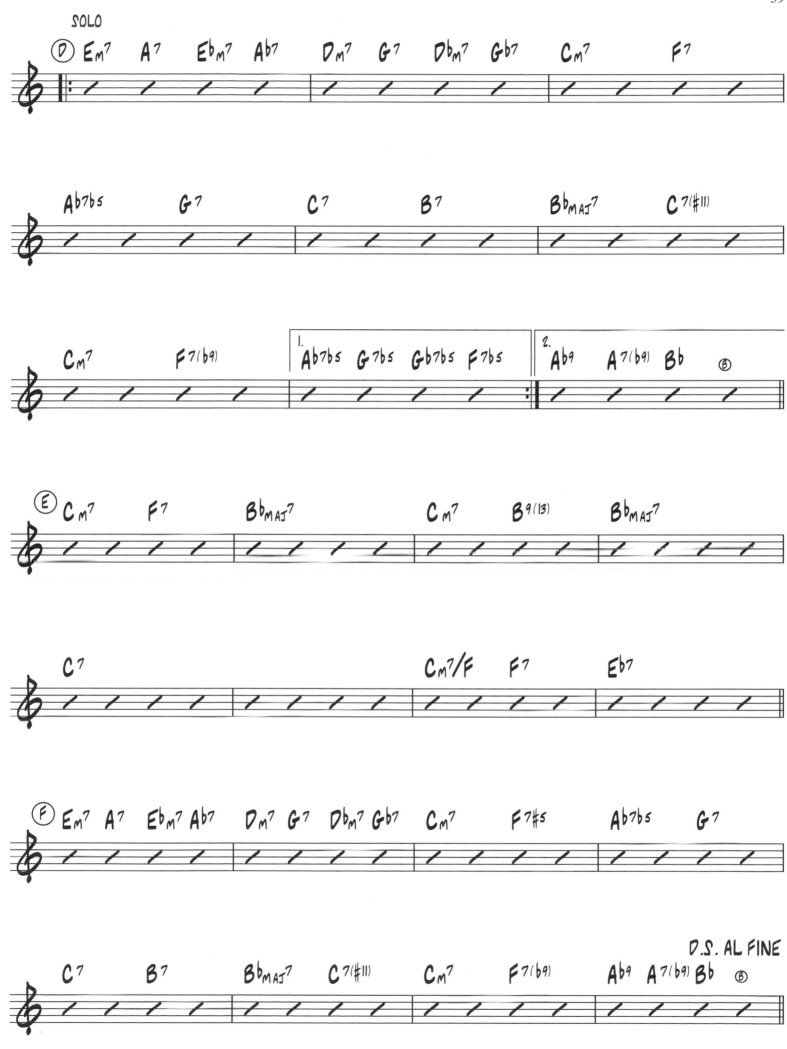

# EVIDENCE

BY THELONIOUS MONK

CD
5: SPLIT TRACK/MELODY
6: FULL STEREO TRACK

Eb VERSION

SOLO (3 CHORUSES)

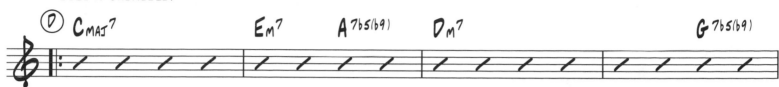

(D) C MAJ7       E M7    A 7b5(b9)    D M7       G 7b5(b9)

F#7b5       F M7    Bb7    D M7       G 7(b9)

(E) G M7       C7       F MAJ7       Bb7

A M7       E 7b5       D 7b5       G 7b5(b9)

(F) C MAJ7       E M7    A 7b5(b9)    D M7       G 7b5(b9)

D.S. AL FINE
(AFTER 3RD CHORUS)

F#7b5       F M7    Bb7    D M7       G 7(b9)

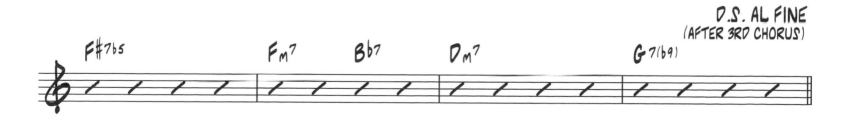

# THINK OF ONE

BY THELONIOUS MONK

Eb VERSION

\* THE 4-NOTE PATTERNS (8TH NOTES) HAVE A MORE EVEN 8TH NOTE FEELING.

SOLO (2 CHORUSES)

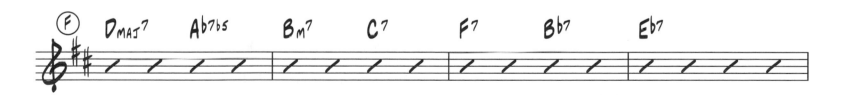

D.S. AL FINE
(AFTER 2ND CHORUS)

D.S. ONLY

# REFLECTIONS

BY THELONIOUS MONK

Eb VERSION

* MONK'S "BENT" NOTE

**CD**

11 : SPLIT TRACK/MELODY
12 : FULL STEREO TRACK

# STRAIGHT NO CHASER

BY THELONIOUS MONK

Eb VERSION

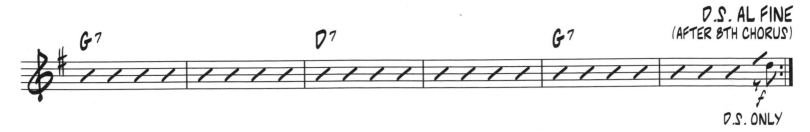

# COMING ON THE HUDSON

BY THELONIOUS MONK

Eb VERSION

# BRAKE'S SAKE

BY THELONIOUS MONK

Eb VERSION

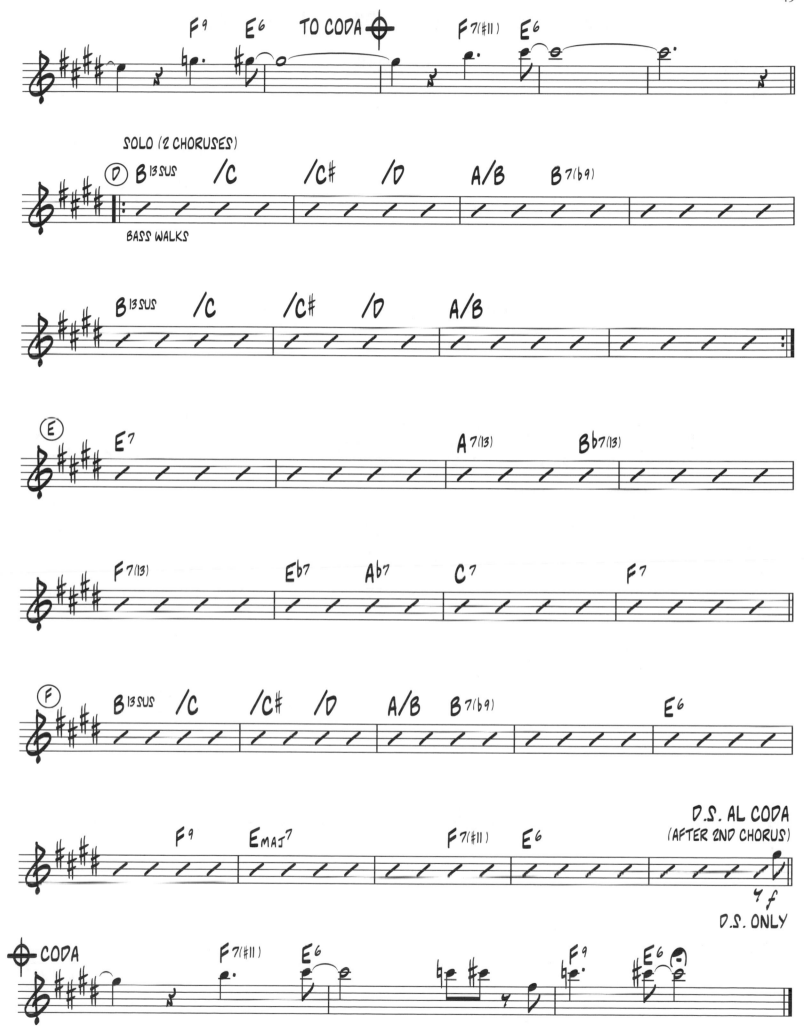

# BA-LUE BOLIVAR BA-LUES-ARE
## (BOLIVAR BLUES)

BY THELONIOUS MONK

# GREEN CHIMNEYS

BY THELONIOUS MONK

# MONK'S DREAM

BY THELONIOUS MONK

# ASK ME NOW

BY THELONIOUS MONK

# EVIDENCE

BY THELONIOUS MONK

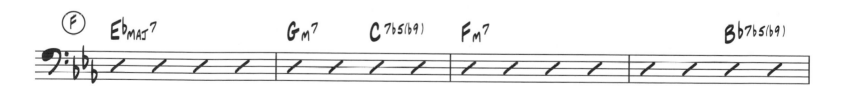

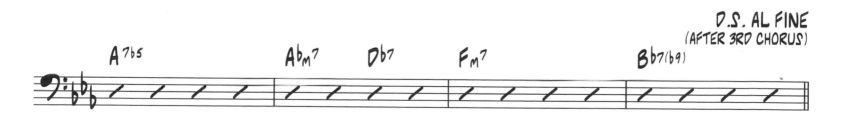

# THINK OF ONE

BY THELONIOUS MONK

\* THE 4-NOTE PATTERNS (8TH NOTES) HAVE A MORE EVEN 8TH NOTE FEELING.

SOLO (2 CHORUSES)

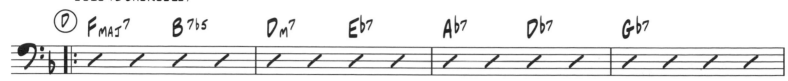

D | F MAJ7 B7b5 | D m7 Eb7 | Ab7 Db7 | Gb7 |

| F MAJ7 B7b5 | D m7 Eb7 | Ab7 | |

Ab7(#9 13)

E | F7 | | Bb MAJ7 | G7(b9) |

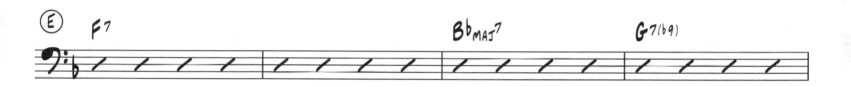

| D m7 | G7b5 | G m7 | C7(#11 b9) |

F | F MAJ7 B7b5 | D m7 Eb7 | Ab7 Db7 | Gb7 |

D.S. AL FINE
(AFTER 2ND CHORUS)

| F MAJ7 B7b5 | D m7 Eb7 | Ab7 | |

Ab7(#9 13)

D.S. ONLY

# REFLECTIONS

BY THELONIOUS MONK

🎼: C VERSION

\* MONK'S "BENT" NOTE

# STRAIGHT NO CHASER

BY THELONIOUS MONK

C VERSION

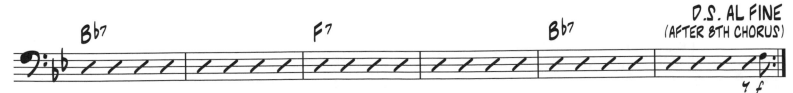

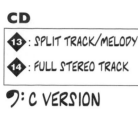

# COMING ON THE HUDSON

BY THELONIOUS MONK

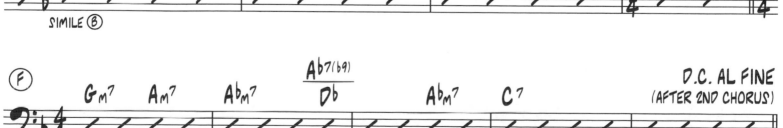

# BRAKE'S SAKE

BY THELONIOUS MONK

𝄢: C VERSION

MEDIUM SWING
INTRO (RHYTHM SECTION)

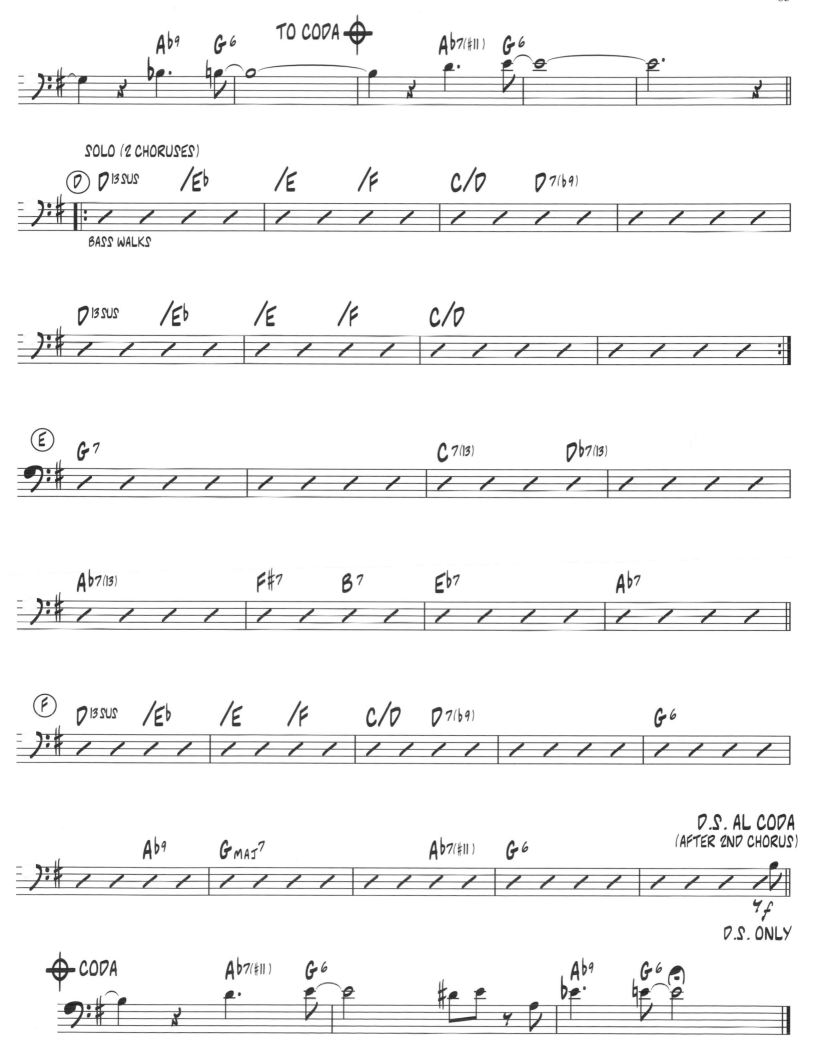

**CD**

# BA-LUE BOLIVAR BA-LUES-ARE
## (BOLIVAR BLUES)

BY THELONIOUS MONK

# GREEN CHIMNEYS

BY THELONIOUS MONK

**CD**
19: SPLIT TRACK/MELODY
20: FULL STEREO TRACK

𝄢: C VERSION

MEDIUM UP SWING
INTRO (SOLO PIANO)

PIANO PLAYS 1ST 8 MEASURES OF Ⓐ FOR THE INTRO

⅏ PLAY
Ⓐ Ab_m

Ⓑ Gb7    Cb7    Gb7    Cb7

Gb7    Cb7    Gb7    Cb7

Ⓒ Ab_m

1. TO SOLO     2. LAST TIME Db7(#11)

SOLO (3 CHORUSES)
Ⓓ Ab_m

Ⓔ Gb7    Cb7    Gb7    Cb7    Gb7    Cb7    Gb7    Cb7

D.S. AL FINE
(AFTER 3RD CHORUS)
Ⓕ Ab_m

**54. "MOONLIGHT IN VERMONT" AND OTHER GREAT STANDARDS**
00843050 .................................$15.99

**55. BENNY GOLSON**
00843052 .................................$15.95

**56. "GEORGIA ON MY MIND" & OTHER SONGS BY HOAGY CARMICHAEL**
00843056 .................................$15.99

**57. VINCE GUARALDI**
00843057 .................................$16.99

**58. MORE LENNON AND MCCARTNEY**
00843059 .................................$15.99

**59. SOUL JAZZ**
00843060 .................................$15.99

**60. DEXTER GORDON**
00843061 .................................$15.95

**61. MONGO SANTAMARIA**
00843062 .................................$15.95

**62. JAZZ-ROCK FUSION**
00843063 .................................$14.95

**63. CLASSICAL JAZZ**
00843064 .................................$14.95

**64. TV TUNES**
00843065 .................................$14.95

**65. SMOOTH JAZZ**
00843066 .................................$16.99

**66. A CHARLIE BROWN CHRISTMAS**
00843067 .................................$16.99

**67. CHICK COREA**
00843068 .................................$15.95

**68. CHARLES MINGUS**
00843069 .................................$16.95

**69. CLASSIC JAZZ**
00843071 .................................$15.99

**70. THE DOORS**
00843072 .................................$14.95

**71. COLE PORTER CLASSICS**
00843073 .................................$14.95

**72. CLASSIC JAZZ BALLADS**
00843074 .................................$15.99

**73. JAZZ/BLUES**
00843075 .................................$14.95

**74. BEST JAZZ CLASSICS**
00843076 .................................$15.99

**75. PAUL DESMOND**
00843077 .................................$14.95

**76. BROADWAY JAZZ BALLADS**
00843078 .................................$15.99

**77. JAZZ ON BROADWAY**
00843079 .................................$15.99

**78. STEELY DAN**
00843070 .................................$14.99

**79. MILES DAVIS CLASSICS**
00843081 .................................$15.99

**80. JIMI HENDRIX**
00843083 .................................$15.99

**81. FRANK SINATRA – CLASSICS**
00843084 .................................$15.99

**82. FRANK SINATRA – STANDARDS**
00843085 .................................$15.99

**83. ANDREW LLOYD WEBBER**
00843104 .................................$14.95

**84. BOSSA NOVA CLASSICS**
00843105 .................................$14.95

**85. MOTOWN HITS**
00843109 .................................$14.95

**86. BENNY GOODMAN**
00843110 .................................$14.95

**87. DIXIELAND**
00843111 .................................$14.95

**88. DUKE ELLINGTON FAVORITES**
00843112 .................................$14.95

**89. IRVING BERLIN FAVORITES**
00843113 .................................$14.95

**90. THELONIOUS MONK CLASSICS**
00841262 .................................$16.99

**91. THELONIOUS MONK FAVORITES**
00841263 .................................$16.99

**92. LEONARD BERNSTEIN**
00450134 .................................$14.99

**93. DISNEY FAVORITES**
00843142 .................................$14.99

**94. RAY**
00843143 .................................$14.95

**95. JAZZ AT THE LOUNGE**
00843144 .................................$14.99

**96. LATIN JAZZ STANDARDS**
00843145 .................................$14.99

**97. MAYBE I'M AMAZED**
00843148 .................................$14.99

**98. DAVE FRISHBERG**
00843149 .................................$15.99

**99. SWINGING STANDARDS**
00843150 .................................$14.99

**100. LOUIS ARMSTRONG**
00740423 .................................$15.99

**101. BUD POWELL**
00843152 .................................$14.99

**102. JAZZ POP**
00843153 .................................$14.99

**103. ON GREEN DOLPHIN STREET & OTHER JAZZ CLASSICS**
00843154 .................................$14.99

**104. ELTON JOHN**
00843155 .................................$14.99

**105. SOULFUL JAZZ**
00843151 .................................$14.99

**106. SLO' JAZZ**
00843117 .................................$14.99

**107. MOTOWN CLASSICS**
00843116 .................................$14.99

**111. COOL CHRISTMAS**
00843162 .................................$15.99

0809

# Jazz Instruction & Improvisation
## Books for All Instruments from Hal Leonard

### AN APPROACH TO JAZZ IMPROVISATION

 **INCLUDES TAB**

*by Dave Pozzi*
Musicians Institute Press
Explore the styles of Charlie Parker, Sonny Rollins, Bud Powell and others with this comprehensive guide to jazz improvisation. Covers: scale choices • chord analysis • phrasing • melodies • harmonic progressions • more.
00695135 Book/CD Pack .......................................$17.95

### BUILDING A JAZZ VOCABULARY

*By Mike Steinel*
A valuable resource for learning the basics of jazz from Mike Steinel of the University of North Texas. It covers: the basics of jazz • how to build effective solos • a comprehensive practice routine • and a jazz vocabulary of the masters.
00849911 ............................................$19.95

### THE CYCLE OF FIFTHS

*by Emile and Laura De Cosmo*
This essential instruction book provides more than 450 exercises, including hundreds of melodic and rhythmic ideas. The book is designed to help improvisors master the cycle of fifths, one of the primary progressions in music. Guaranteed to refine technique, enhance improvisational fluency, and improve sight-reading!
00311114 ............................................$16.99

### THE DIATONIC CYCLE

*by Emile and Laura De Cosmo*
Renowned jazz educators Emile and Laura De Cosmo provide more than 300 exercises to help improvisors tackle one of music's most common progressions: the diatonic cycle. This book is guaranteed to refine technique, enhance improvisational fluency, and improve sight-reading!
00311115 ............................................$16.95

### EAR TRAINING

*by Keith Wyatt, Carl Schroeder and Joe Elliott*
Musicians Institute Press
Covers: basic pitch matching • singing major and minor scales • identifying intervals • transcribing melodies and rhythm • identifying chords and progressions • seventh chords and the blues • modal interchange, chromaticism, modulation • and more.
00695198 Book/2-CD Pack....................................$24.95

### EXERCISES AND ETUDES FOR THE JAZZ INSTRUMENTALIST

*by J.J. Johnson*
Designed as study material and playable by any instrument, these pieces run the gamut of the jazz experience, featuring common and uncommon time signatures and keys, and styles from ballads to funk. They are progressively graded so that both beginners and professionals will be challenged by the demands of this wonderful music.
00842018 Bass Clef Edition.................................$16.95
00842042 Treble Clef Edition ...............................$16.95

### JAZZOLOGY

THE ENCYCLOPEDIA OF JAZZ THEORY FOR ALL MUSICIANS
*by Robert Rawlins and Nor Eddine Bahha*
This comprehensive resource covers a variety of jazz topics, for beginners and pros of any instrument. The book serves as an encyclopedia for reference, a thorough methodology for the student, and a workbook for the classroom.
00311167 ............................................$18.95

### JAZZ THEORY RESOURCES

*by Bert Ligon*
Houston Publishing, Inc.
This is a jazz theory text in two volumes. **Volume 1 includes:** review of basic theory • rhythm in jazz performance • triadic generalization • diatonic harmonic progressions and analysis • substitutions and turnarounds • and more. **Volume 2 includes:** modes and modal frameworks • quartal harmony • extended tertian structures and triadic superimposition • pentatonic applications • coloring "outside" the lines and beyond • and more.
00030458 Volume 1 ...............................$39.95
00030459 Volume 2 ...............................$29.95

### JOY OF IMPROV

*by Dave Frank and John Amaral*
This book/CD course on improvisation for all instruments and all styles will help players develop monster musical skills! **Book One** imparts a solid basis in technique, rhythm, chord theory, ear training and improv concepts. **Book Two** explores more advanced chord voicings, chord arranging techniques and more challenging blues and melodic lines. The CD can be used as a listening and play-along tool.
00220005 Book 1 – Book/CD Pack ......................$24.95
00220006 Book 2 – Book/CD Pack ......................$24.95

### THE PATH TO JAZZ IMPROVISATION

*by Emile and Laura De Cosmo*
This fascinating jazz instruction book offers an innovative, scholarly approach to the art of improvisation. It includes in-depth analysis and lessons about: cycle of fifths • diatonic cycle • overtone series • pentatonic scale • harmonic and melodic minor scale • polytonal order of keys • blues and bebop scales • modes • and more.
00310904 ............................................$14.95

### THE SOURCE

THE DICTIONARY OF CONTEMPORARY AND TRADITIONAL SCALES
*by Steve Barta*
This book serves as an informative guide for people who are looking for good, solid information regarding scales, chords, and how they work together. It provides right and left hand fingerings for scales, chords, and complete inversions. Includes over 20 different scales, each written in all 12 keys.
00240885 ............................................$15.95

### 21 BEBOP EXERCISES

*by Steve Rawlins*
This book/CD pack is both a warm-up collection and a manual for bebop phrasing. Its tasty and sophisticated exercises will help you develop your proficiency with jazz interpretation. It concentrates on practice in all twelve keys – moving higher by half-step – to help develop dexterity and range. The companion CD includes all of the exercises in 12 keys.
00315341 Book/CD Pack ......................................$17.95

### THE WOODSHEDDING SOURCE BOOK

*by Emile De Cosmo*
Rehearsing with this method daily will improve technique, reading ability, rhythmic and harmonic vocabulary, eye/finger coordination, endurance, range, theoretical knowledge, and listening skills – all of which lead to superior improvisational skills.
00842000 C Instruments........................................$19.95

FOR MORE INFORMATION, SEE YOUR LOCAL MUSIC DEALER, OR WRITE TO:

**HAL•LEONARD®**
CORPORATION
7777 W. BLUEMOUND RD. P.O. BOX 13819 MILWAUKEE, WI 53213

Prices, contents & availability subject to change without notice.

Visit Hal Leonard online at
**www.halleonard.com**

0409

# ARTIST TRANSCRIPTIONS

Artist Transcriptions are authentic, note-for-note transcriptions of today's hottest artists in jazz, pop and rock. These outstanding, accurate arrangements are in an easy-to-read format which includes all essential lines. Artist Transcriptions can be used to perform, sequence or for reference.

## CLARINET

| | | |
|---|---|---|
| 00672423 | Buddy De Franco Collection | $19.95 |

## FLUTE

| | | |
|---|---|---|
| 00672379 | Eric Dolphy Collection | $19.95 |
| 00672372 | James Moody Collection – Sax and Flute | $19.95 |
| 00660108 | James Newton – Improvising Flute | $14.95 |
| 00672455 | Lew Tabackin Collection | $19.95 |

## GUITAR & BASS

| | | |
|---|---|---|
| 00660113 | The Guitar Style of George Benson | $14.95 |
| 00699072 | Guitar Book of Pierre Bensusan | $29.95 |
| 00672331 | Ron Carter – Acoustic Bass | $16.95 |
| 00672307 | Stanley Clarke Collection | $19.95 |
| 00660115 | Al Di Meola – Friday Night in San Francisco | $14.95 |
| 00604043 | Al Di Meola – Music, Words, Pictures | $14.95 |
| 00673245 | Jazz Style of Tal Farlow | $19.95 |
| 00672359 | Bela Fleck and the Flecktones | $18.95 |
| 00699389 | Jim Hall – Jazz Guitar Environments | $19.95 |
| 00699306 | Jim Hall – Exploring Jazz Guitar | $19.95 |
| 00604049 | Allan Holdsworth – Reaching for the Uncommon Chord | $14.95 |
| 00699215 | Leo Kottke – Eight Songs | $14.95 |
| 00672356 | Jazz Guitar Standards | $19.95 |
| 00675536 | Wes Montgomery – Guitar Transcriptions | $17.95 |
| 00672353 | Joe Pass Collection | $18.95 |
| 00673216 | John Patitucci | $16.95 |
| 00027083 | Django Reinhardt Antholog | $14.95 |
| 00026711 | Genius of Django Reinhardt | $10.95 |
| 00026715 | Django Reinhardt - A Treasury of Songs | $12.95 |
| 00672374 | Johnny Smith Guitar Solos | $16.95 |
| 00672320 | Mark Whitfield | $19.95 |

## PIANO & KEYBOARD

| | | |
|---|---|---|
| 00672338 | Monty Alexander Collection | $19.95 |
| 00672487 | Monty Alexander Plays Standards | $19.95 |
| 00672318 | Kenny Barron Collection | $22.95 |
| 00672520 | Count Basie Collection | $19.95 |
| 00672364 | Warren Bernhardt Collection | $19.95 |
| 00672439 | Cyrus Chestnut Collection | $19.95 |
| 00673242 | Billy Childs Collection | $19.95 |
| 00672300 | Chick Corea – Paint the World | $12.95 |
| 00672537 | Bill Evans at Town Hall | $16.95 |
| 00672425 | Bill Evans – Piano Interpretations | $19.95 |
| 00672365 | Bill Evans – Piano Standards | $19.95 |
| 00672510 | Bill Evans Trio – Vol. 1: 1959-1961 | $24.95 |
| 00672511 | Bill Evans Trio – Vol. 2: 1962-1965 | $24.95 |
| 00672512 | Bill Evans Trio – Vol. 3: 1968-1974 | $24.95 |
| 00672513 | Bill Evans Trio – Vol. 4: 1979-1980 | $24.95 |
| 00672381 | Tommy Flanagan Collection | $19.95 |
| 00672492 | Benny Goodman Collection | $16.95 |
| 00672329 | Benny Green Collection | $19.95 |

| | | |
|---|---|---|
| 00672486 | Vince Guaraldi Collection | $19.95 |
| 00672419 | Herbie Hancock Collection | $19.95 |
| 00672438 | Hampton Hawes | $19.95 |
| 00672322 | Ahmad Jamal Collection | $22.95 |
| 00672476 | Brad Mehldau Collection | $19.95 |
| 00672388 | Best of Thelonious Monk | $19.95 |
| 00672389 | Thelonious Monk Collection | $19.95 |
| 00672390 | Thelonious Monk Plays Jazz Standards – Volume 1 | $19.95 |
| 00672391 | Thelonious Monk Plays Jazz Standards – Volume 2 | $19.95 |
| 00672433 | Jelly Roll Morton – The Piano Rolls | $12.95 |
| 00672553 | Charlie Parker for Piano | $19.95 |
| 00672542 | Oscar Peterson – Jazz Piano Solos | $16.95 |
| 00672544 | Oscar Peterson – Originals | $9.95 |
| 00672532 | Oscar Peterson – Plays Broadway | $19.95 |
| 00672531 | Oscar Peterson – Plays Duke Ellington | $19.95 |
| 00672533 | Oscar Peterson – Trios | $24.95 |
| 00672543 | Oscar Peterson Trio – Canadiana Suite | $9.95 |
| 00672534 | Very Best of Oscar Peterson | $22.95 |
| 00672371 | Bud Powell Classics | $19.95 |
| 00672376 | Bud Powell Collection | $19.95 |
| 00672437 | André Previn Collection | $19.95 |
| 00672507 | Gonzalo Rubalcaba Collection | $19.95 |
| 00672303 | Horace Silver Collection | $19.95 |
| 00672316 | Art Tatum Collection | $22.95 |
| 00672355 | Art Tatum Solo Book | $19.95 |
| 00672357 | Billy Taylor Collection | $24.95 |
| 00673215 | McCoy Tyner | $16.95 |
| 00672321 | Cedar Walton Collection | $19.95 |
| 00672519 | Kenny Werner Collection | $19.95 |
| 00672434 | Teddy Wilson Collection | $19.95 |

## SAXOPHONE

| | | |
|---|---|---|
| 00673244 | Julian "Cannonball" Adderley Collection | $19.95 |
| 00673237 | Michael Brecker | $19.95 |
| 00672429 | Michael Brecker Collection | $19.95 |
| 00672447 | Best of the Brecker Brothers | $19.95 |
| 00672315 | Benny Carter Plays Standards | $22.95 |
| 00672314 | Benny Carter Collection | $22.95 |
| 00672394 | James Carter Collection | $19.95 |
| 00672349 | John Coltrane Plays Giant Steps | $19.95 |
| 00672529 | John Coltrane – Giant Steps | $14.95 |
| 00672494 | John Coltrane – A Love Supreme | $14.95 |
| 00672493 | John Coltrane Plays "Coltrane Changes" | $19.95 |
| 00672453 | John Coltrane Plays Standards | $19.95 |
| 00673233 | John Coltrane Solos | $22.95 |
| 00672328 | Paul Desmond Collection | $19.95 |
| 00672379 | Eric Dolphy Collection | $19.95 |
| 00672530 | Kenny Garrett Collection | $19.95 |
| 00699375 | Stan Getz | $19.95 |
| 00672377 | Stan Getz – Bossa Novas | $19.95 |
| 00672375 | Stan Getz – Standards | $18.95 |
| 00673254 | Great Tenor Sax Solos | $18.95 |
| 00672523 | Coleman Hawkins Collection | $19.95 |

| | | |
|---|---|---|
| 00673252 | Joe Henderson – Selections from "Lush Life" & "So Near So Far" | $19.95 |
| 00672330 | Best of Joe Henderson | $22.95 |
| 00673239 | Best of Kenny G | $19.95 |
| 00673229 | Kenny G – Breathless | $19.95 |
| 00672462 | Kenny G – Classics in the Key of G | $19.95 |
| 00672485 | Kenny G – Faith: A Holiday Album | $14.95 |
| 00672373 | Kenny G – The Moment | $19.95 |
| 00672326 | Joe Lovano Collection | $19.95 |
| 00672498 | Jackie McLean Collection | $19.95 |
| 00672372 | James Moody Collection – Sax and Flute | $19.95 |
| 00672416 | Frank Morgan Collection | $19.95 |
| 00672539 | Gerry Mulligan Collection | $19.95 |
| 00672352 | Charlie Parker Collection | $19.95 |
| 00672561 | Best of Sonny Rollins | $19.95 |
| 00672444 | Sonny Rollins Collection | $19.95 |
| 00675000 | David Sanborn Collection | $17.95 |
| 00672528 | Bud Shank Collection | $19.95 |
| 00672491 | New Best of Wayne Shorter | $19.95 |
| 00672455 | Lew Tabackin Collection | $19.95 |
| 00672350 | Tenor Saxophone Standards | $18.95 |
| 00672334 | Stanley Turrentine Collection | $19.95 |
| 00672524 | Lester Young Collection | $19.95 |

## TROMBONE

| | | |
|---|---|---|
| 00672332 | J.J. Johnson Collection | $19.95 |
| 00672489 | Steve Turré Collection | $19.95 |

## TRUMPET

| | | |
|---|---|---|
| 00672557 | Herb Alpert Collection | $14.95 |
| 00672480 | Louis Armstrong Collection | $17.95 |
| 00672481 | Louis Armstrong Plays Standards | $17.95 |
| 00672435 | Chet Baker Collection | $19.95 |
| 00672556 | Best of Chris Botti | $19.95 |
| 00673234 | Randy Brecker | $17.95 |
| 00672447 | Best of the Brecker Brothers | $19.95 |
| 00672448 | Miles Davis – Originals, Vol. 1 | $19.95 |
| 00672451 | Miles Davis – Originals, Vol. 2 | $19.95 |
| 00672450 | Miles Davis – Standards, Vol. 1 | $19.95 |
| 00672449 | Miles Davis – Standards, Vol. 2 | $19.95 |
| 00672479 | Dizzy Gillespie Collection | $19.95 |
| 00673214 | Freddie Hubbard | $14.95 |
| 00672382 | Tom Harrell – Jazz Trumpet | $19.95 |
| 00672363 | Jazz Trumpet Solos | $9.95 |
| 00672506 | Chuck Mangione Collection | $19.95 |
| 00672525 | Arturo Sandoval – Trumpet Evolution | $19.95 |

FOR MORE INFORMATION, SEE YOUR LOCAL MUSIC DEALER, OR WRITE TO:

HAL•LEONARD® CORPORATION
7777 W. BLUEMOUND RD. P.O. BOX 13819 MILWAUKEE, WI 53213

**Visit our web site for a complete listing of our titles with songlists at**
**www.halleonard.com**

Prices and availability subject to change without notice.

1208